How to Meditate- *easily*

It sounds simple. Right?
Well, if you are one of those people
that have tried it and have had no luck
or so you think, I'm here to guide you.

It is kinda difficult if you *try* too hard.
Trying is the best way *not to* meditate.
I say this because you will be **thinking**
of how to do it. **Thinking how** is
distracting you.
Meditation is very different than you
think because **Meditation is Mindless.**
 Now, don't take that as meaning
being stupid. **I mean it as *not***
thinking, not worrying, not expecting.

I bet you heard about methods of meditating. Most tell you to *relax and suggest* that you empty your mind.
If that is how they are *telling* you to meditate it doesn't seem very helpful.

I am going to teach you by showing you. I will share with you the best and easiest techniques. You can choose one or more ways that resonate with you. You will *actually feel how* by associating with the relatable visuals and stories I share.
 If you tried to *empty your mind* and weren't given an explanation how to do it- I can clear that up for you.

First of all, that advice is not total bull, but *what if* you don't know what the term *clear your mind* really means? Does that mean take a vacuum cleaner and hold it up to my ears?

Let me help ya- *not* with the vacuum of course-

I have been meditating since I was a child, but I didn't know it. I feel that many of you have been doing the same-*not realizing* it.

I *realized* I was meditating about 10 years ago. The understanding of how and why made me continue daily.

Once you realize what meditating

does for you and how your body feels
during and after-you will be hooked.

I did find that in the last 10 years of
my life that I was actually over
meditating. Yeah, I said over
meditating **not** over medicating! Who
knew it could be automatic?

Are you thinking, is that a bad thing?
The answer is not really. However, a
person needs to be more *present* in
the moment too. That's kind of why I
feel we are all here on Earth. Being
present is noticing and having
awareness of those occurrences in
life.

I was daydreaming 24/7. Some

people label that as a negative symptom, but frankly it's just exactly that – I was meditating too much! Some also believe this is a term called "out of your head, or too floaty, or not grounded." The action of meditating doesn't mean we cannot be grounded while meditating.   I will explain this in many examples coming up in this book.

Okay, back to easily meditating.

First of all, there are several avenues to get you to that Zen place. It is a state of mind. But how do you know when you are there?

I have had many people ask me: *how can I meditate and just be?*

I want to be a smart ass and say "be" what? But instead, I gracefully share the following methods.

I've taught thousands of people how to meditate and relax in several of my classes and workshops. I had to be creative on explaining to people of all ages how to meditate. Describing *how* to do it was the challenge. I wanted my students to accept the words I used to describe this ***"process of mindlessness."*** – Yeah that what I call it- Mind*less*ness. It's not meant in a negative way. Well, at least not in this context I'm using for this meditation book.

Truthfully, it's not at all about learning a method. It is mainly about *feeling*. I can explain it simply. Here's the drum roll, the big secret…

Meditation is when you forget about "time". Yep.
Place that cell phone, that clock far, far away.
 Hmm I bet it's already different than you thought. I'll continue.
Time is what keeps us thinking. It makes us think of *what* we should do,

how we should do it and *when*. It also makes us feel that certain places and things need to be categorized. Plus **where** and **when** *all of these things should be* accomplished.

On top of all that thinking, you are trying to decide if you really want to do all those tasks--or not!

No wonder your mind is so active! Busy, busy, busy, sometimes our minds are busier than our bodies doing these actions. A hamster wheel comes to my mind. **Over thinking** can be a bitch. Round and round ya go, just **stop that thought of a task** and let it go!

Let go? How? Start with this. Get a notepad and a pen. Write down those things that were in your head. Those thoughts that were going round and round in your head- like the hamster wheel. I know, I know, you say you cannot stop thinking of them because if you do, you will forget to do all those things and some of it is work that you get paid to do.

Yeah, yeah, I heard that before. Just do it. No excuses-write the things and thoughts down on paper.

A little FYI- inside scoop. If you hold on to all that stuff, most-likely- you have some deeper stuff going on.

You may feel the need to hold on to all those tasks and responsibilities because it makes you feel important, or "needed" by others. I am not saying this is all of you. Some of you are just busy people and have businesses and all that going on. But if you notice you continually can't let go of overthinking, it's a pattern! That means you need to look deeper and fill that void in your life- sit and evaluate what that might be for you. Okay this is getting into another whole different ball game. I am just sayin'. It may be you have a fear of "losing control" of yourself. If this sounds a bit like you, I would like to share a mantra (something you can repeat daily to help you).

The mantra: **"Meditation is simply relaxing. Only I can control me- I allow myself to relax. I can relax my mind and my body."**

Just say it for giggles.

Here is another mantra to say:

" I am important. I allow myself to relax my mind and body. I will remain important."

Moving on. Once you write *all that stuff* in your thoughts, including that list of things to do-down on paper, you won't have to hold them in the

hamster wheel of overthinking.
Because you can pick up that paper
later and read them! Trust me- you
will not forget all those things. You
have them written to remind you.
 Cabesh? Good. For few moments *you*
can stop the hamster wheel that is
holding those tasks and duties.

If you are not on board yet-

Here is how to let go of all of those
thoughts another way- it **_is_** easy.
Now, you are saying – bulls#*#.
Hear me friends.
 The concept of **time** is what you have
to let fly away.

Listen to these ways you can forget about time.

Most of you have probably done a task- let me use the example of driving a car. At first when you learned how, it took a bit of time to get used to. You learned all the rules on the road, how the gas petal and the brake worked, then learning the turn signals, signage etc. Let's say now it's 3 years later, you can drive mindlessly. Meaning not bad, but kind of like you are on *auto pilot*.

You just perform the motions without *thinking*. You are driving! Next thing you know, you are at a destination.

I am **not condoning** you to meditate while driving. It happens and I am using this example because I feel we all can relate.

I know you are starting to get-it. Aren't you?

Next example; this is for those that love gardening out there. It's a wonderful day and you have purchased some beautiful flowers for your garden. You have all your tools and potting soil. You are ready to plant some seeds or flowers in the ground. It becomes second nature; you automatically just do the task. It could be 10, 15 minutes or much more *time* but **you enjoyed that without thinking about the process to do it.**

Years ago I was in the flower business. I owned a flower shop and designed beautiful roses, orchids, hydrangeas, daises, you name it, and I designed them into beautiful creations of art. I would start by gathering all the items I needed to start my flower project. The next thing I knew my mother whom helped me often, walked into the back of the flower shop where I had been designing and said "Jolie- its 8pm at night! You have been designing flowers for 6 hours. Don't you know what time it is?" I was lost in an abyss; I couldn't tell you where my mind went. But I don't remember holding the clippers or making the 20 arrangements that were in front of me. I *loved* to design flowers. It made me happy where nothing else mattered around me. I guess you can say it was a passion of mine.

Now I am not saying you can't meditate while sitting in a crossed legged position... but it is not the only way. An absolutely quiet space is great and certainly can help meditation, but is not necessarily the only factor to do it. Some people are more relaxed in a nosier atmosphere- just because they are used to that type of environment. I have friend that lived in NYC and the noise never stopped. She came to visit me in Florida and found it made her crazy because it was just too quiet.

My point is to find your comfort zone. This can be your space-a location. This is a comfort zone or place that helps you feel relaxed. If it's going for a run through noisy New York by all means get in that space!

I am showing you many ways you can

meditate because most of us do it already. You didn't understand that what you were/are doing can already be a form of meditation.

Passion & Love

Start by thinking about what you really love to do. Things you actually mark out time in your busy week to do. Having passion for an action you do is healthy.

Sometimes just visualizing and thinking about those *nice experiences* get you there in your mind. I call this the beginning of **mind space**.

Mind space starts with that thought of happiness that becomes stronger and stronger until all you feel in your body is *that happiness*. It is that bliss- that visual or feeling of that. It could be a vision, object, thing or thought of that happy happy, joy joy.

It can be felt in your psychical body or just imagined by you- or none of the above which is **mind space. This is the not knowing of what you were thinking or feeling.** Trust me it's good for you.

There are *no rules* with meditation. So- stop *overthinking* there are! **Let's use another example of** meditation.

Do you love working out with weights? Or running?

Let use the runner's high explanation. If you ever enjoyed running and found after a certain point you felt incredible. It was not a struggle to keep running. That "high" is meditation. You stopped thinking and just got to the enjoyment of it. The bliss. No words needed.

Cooking is another great meditation. Have you ever cooked mindlessly and found that there was a great meal on the plate in front of you? You forgot about time and just **did the task without thinking.**

Levels of Meditation

There are different levels of meditation and where the mind "goes". How deep can you go? The answer is DEEP.

Below I give you Wikipedia's defining terms on the levels of brainwaves humans have. I then, give you *my easy* understanding of them.

An altered level of consciousness is any measure of arousal other than normal. Level of consciousness (LOC) is a measurement of a person's arousability and responsiveness to stimuli from the environment.

Theta state of mind - tends to appear during meditative, drowsy, or sleeping states, but not during the deepest stages of sleep. Beta - beta brain waves during REM sleep that are associated with wakefulness. The .Delta-A delta wave is a high amplitude brain wave with a frequency of oscillation between 0–4 hertz. Delta waves, like other brain waves, are recorded with an electroencephalogram[1] (EEG) and are usually associated with the deep stage 3 of NREM sleep, also known as slow-wave sleep (SWS), and aid in characterizing the depth of sleep. Wikipedia

Simplicity

My understanding of the brainwave levels simply put:

1.deep

2.deeper

3. **Super** deep- out of this world. Also known as **MIND SPACE**.

The deeper we are in the meditation the closer you are to mind space.

There is so much out there on the web you can explore. Many people express what they feel from each meditation. Some people share colorful images, signs or graphics. Including places they have never been to but visually feel or see. They claim they see these locations in their minds. There are tons of comparable materials out there. From simple to outrageous experiences, YouTube is the mecca.

I found that sometimes all of that information can be confusing or overwhelming. Please don't compare or feel turned off due to some nuts out there. Meditation is beautiful. Just relax with one of the ways I explained- or be inspired from a meditation practice that you feel comfortable exploring.

This way you won't over expect. You won't feel that if you are not getting or feeling *what those people* felt or visualized- that you are doing it wrong.

This is all you need to know:

THERE IS NO WRONG WAY TO MEDITATE.

NO RULES.

THERE IS NO TIME.

ONLY YOU CAN DECIDE TO GO TO

THE LOVING SPACE.

FIND THE HAPPY PLACE OR

MIND SPACE.

It's not what you think or do not think about.

It- is how your body feels that can get you to mind space.

Follow my lead...

When you forget about time you are in a meditation state.

Tips for Meditating:

Do this- without trying too hard!

It's like listening to a person speak to you but not hearing them. I think you know what I mean. Tune out. By the way none of us are saints! We have all tuned someone out at some point in our lives.

1. Focusing on your body. Pick one area on your body- now focus on it.

2. Focusing on sound. Hear it, and then lose yourself in that sound or vibrational flow. Focus on one instrument or beat within the music. Sound can raise the levels of the consciousness.

I know realistically some of you don't know what the word consciousness means. It means being aware of ones surroundings. So how does it make you more aware *without* thinking you ask?

Well, it's like the word I use a lot. The word is *mindful*. **Being mindful is sensing *or* to understand you and what is affected by you**. That is the Jolie definition.

About sound-sound can raise your consciousness to better understandings of the mind space. This is bringing you to a state of an AhHAA moment. This way you can be in mind space, but also have epiphanies without thinking.

I know it sounds like an oxymoron an opposite thing- by the way I love that word. I am laughing out loud, but it truly can happen. Some people also call this *"enlightenment."* It's like when you don't focus and get a brilliant vision pop into you and you are wondering how the heck YOU got

that brilliant idea five minutes later.
It's like that.

Here's the other tip. Remember the idea of the focusing on the body? Choosing one area of the body and zoning into feel that area and notice it. Do that.

It is easy to focus on colors or your own body.
This keeps you focused on one thing not 5 trillion other things. Whenever you start thinking of you grocery lists or chores bring your focus back on to that body part or you can imagine a color.

You actually can focus on an area of your body and a color- I know. I know. Now you have to think about that! NO! Don't.

Just visualize it once. Use the helpful picture in this book. It is right here on the next page. This way you can see the colors and where on your body they correlate.

Body area & color meditation

 Start by imagining both **1)** choose your body part- or focus on the center of your chest. This is easy for everyone to visualize. This location on the body is also known as the heart chakra. **2)** Now visualize and imagine the color green at the same time.

3) Now imagine feeling your body without touching it physically. Just notice that area with focusing your *thought*- at the center of your chest.

4) Imagine a green light in that spot and start to feel or visualize your happy place or passion for something you love. Good. You got it.

If you practice that technique, you will *not* have to think about it. Ya know, like driving that car mindlessly. The actions just happen.

When you imagine the green light and the spot on your body, you are keeping your focus on you .This keeps the mind chatter out. No hamster wheels are allowed here.

Here is a picture you can visualize when sitting to meditate:

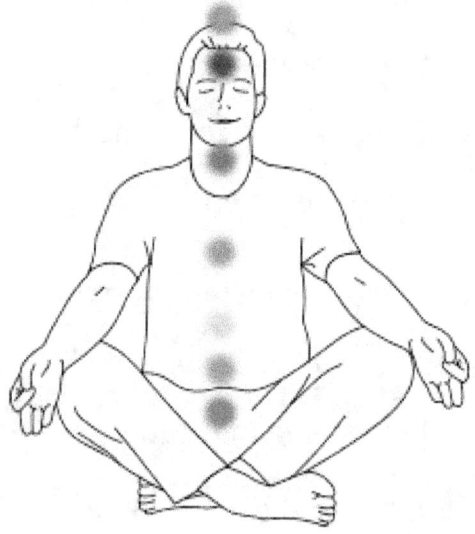

In learning of meditations or in practices such as yoga you will hear people talk of **chakras.** This is a majical word. *Just kidding.* It is cool to say, but the idea is that these chakras are energetic wheels with colors that certainly help you get to that mindless state. Check out the next pages for details.

The 7 main energy centers called Chakra points

are as shown in this picture supplied by clip art.

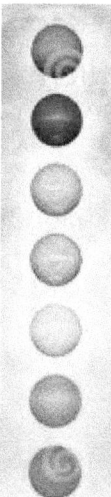

CHAKRAS

Chakras are energy centers that are located down the center of a person's body along the meridian or spinal column. These wheel or disc-like centers is also associated with colors for each chakra point. There are 7 main chakras but there are over 144,000 chakras in the human body. Pretty cool Hugh? These are energy centers that constantly open and close on a day to day basis.

They can also change every time you have a positive or negative thought.

 Each chakra represents a center point in the human body which can energize, release, hold or vibrate. These energy centers constantly open and close during the day. This is normal, but keeping them balanced is the key to being a balanced human. It can be compared to the concept of the human ego. We never see it by *everyone* in the world talks about it. It is silly because we don't have to let go or diminish our ego's to be happy. We simply need to balance it!

When I say balanced, I mean physically, mentally, emotionally and spiritually balanced. It is easy; we can do it with our thoughts. Then those thoughts adjust our feelings and perceptions. Easy- super easy!

When we humans (I said- *we*) are unbalanced in any one of these areas they can be over compensating in another area of the body. If a chakra is out of place- for a long period of time, sickness can manifest. This could be as physical, mental, emotional or spiritual. This proves keeping *yourself* and your energy centers/chakras aligned and balanced is a must.

The chakra at the base of the spine is called the **root or 1st chakra**. This chakra represents *grounding*, being in the now and wanting to be on Earth.

The **2nd chakra is named the sacral** - representing survival, instinct. The **3rd chakra is solar plexus** representing personal power, your emotions and/ or your EGO.

The **4th chakra -the heart** area represents love and compassion. The **5th chakra is the throat** chakra representing communication, expression, and creativeness. It also represents being heard by other people or not. As well as being expressive of speaking your truth.

The 6th chakra represents the third eye or mind's eye. This is your intuition and trusting in yourself.

Lastly is the **7th chakra**- which represents connection to your higher self and crown of your head. Some feel the connection to energies of light, your source- whom your belief system recognizes as a higher power. Some believe in the *higher –self-* as the all-knowing part of you. You can also connect with the celestial plane of Angels, your Source, Spirit guides, and humans that have passed over or on other dimensions. You can do this by simply stating your intention. The intention would be- *that you would like their presence in your meditation.*

If this chakra stuff freaks you out a bit, just do the focus on the body part technique.

Different strokes for different folks- but all meditations are great to reduce stress and lower blood pressure along with benefits of prolonging life.

The more you know about your body the more it can help you stay balanced. It is a good energy exchange that balances you on the physical, emotional and mental levels. Taking good care of your physical body is part of the exchange as well. You most likely feel healthier *or better* when you eat foods that are known as natural or organic, basically unprocessed. That is a positive energy exchange with your insides and outside on the physical level.

Your chakras are the example of the perfect energy exchange on an energetic level. Again if that was TMI (too much information) on the chakras and energy, it's okay.

Move on to the other techniques. You are too close to mastering this meditation thing!

Synchronicity

The human aura works in synchronicity with our energy centers. Chakras and auras work together for balancing our bodies. You will find a 20 minute meditation session is a healthy, alternative method for cleansing the energy in one's body. Think of it as a monthly maintenance.

One method is using a form of *energy healing* to keep our bodies' aura clean and clear. This clarity keeps us aligned and balanced to feel great.

There are many types of energy healing modalities that cleanse our bodies. Reiki is a Japanese modality where the body is a used as conduit. The body is utilized as a pipe- to flow this unlimited energy that comes from a universal source. This can be a source of whomever or whatever your belief system derives from. Universal source or named sources such as Buddha, God, Jah, Angels, or Earth.

Doing a *self-meditation or voice guided meditation* is beneficial to balance and heal your energy system. You can be balance your mind, physical body and energetic body (the aura) easily within 20 minutes. When doing a self-meditation, guided meditation or receiving Reiki –can positively re- align and balance your chakras. Basically these modalities can assist in cleaning your auric field. Remember -your aura is also known as your energy body abbreviated as **EMF**- the electromagnetic field that surrounds your human body. We cannot visually see this energy field, however some talented humans can. I can! I can!

Actually, we all can see and feel them! It just takes practice.

The aura is our part of us that is connected to our physical body, but unseen to most human's eyes. Nevertheless we all can feel and sense with it. Just for fun, notice how much you feel from other people without asking them what is going on in their lives. Just stand next to a person and notice if you feel anything from their aura. For those of you that can be really intense in your learning processes, please don't make anyone feel uncomfortable by doing this. Remember your manners and respect others!

 One way to balance you within 5 minutes is this **Rainbow self –healing** technique. Imagine a rainbow of beautiful colors, all hues. Then imagine all those amazing colors washing over your entire body from the top of your head to the bottoms of your feet. Then say verbally - *anything other than the light will go out of your body and energy field into the earth to be recycled and renewed.* YOU did it! You are clean and clear. By the way, in my world if *you* can visualize a colorful rainbow- *you are going to be* successful at anything you set your mind to!

Another meditation exercise I like to do to is called a relaxing *test* of feeling *thyself.*

I know- I know- it totally sounds perverted- it is *not that at all*.

I promise.

I start by sitting comfortably then saying these certain words to myself. These particular words give me a wide variety of emotions. For instance, I would say aloud "love." Then I would say internally "love."

You can repeat them a few times and

feel as if your body is getting lighter. I really feel that good vibe energy!

You are raising your physical and energy body's vibration. It makes me feel elated or feel as if I am escalating my energy. This means my physical body and my energy body / aura is on a higher frequency which just means good!

When I say the word which is a vibration from the inner mind and then verbally say the word out loud – I feel balanced. I am balanced inside and out! Here are more words I say inner and outwardly. I do it all in one 15 minute sitting. If you forget about the words after you start, just keep feeling and *unthinking*. Feel free to forget about time as well. It is great! You can say the words slow or fast, but repeat them a few times each and see how your energy feels afterwards.

Gratitude

Happy

Laughter

Sweet

Healthy

Beautiful.

You might **feel** some of these words stronger than others as you say them aloud or within. Now try to connect to each part of your body. You can also just pick on section of your body you find easiest to focus on. As you express the words- notice again each different section of your physical body. You will notice **where** in your body you feel the most.

For example: When I would say the word *laughter* in my mind, then aloud- I feel it in my throat area the most.

Take a mental note of where you feel the word you choose to say. It can be very telling of what is going on with you and in your life.

Here is what I call noticeable action.

This is an exercise to relax.

Opening your mind to new possibilities is more than saying words– but is doing "action" to that thought.

Many of us go to work, come home and worry about all the things we need to do or have to get done. Take a moment– allow 2 minutes -breathe in and out slowly, then ask yourself:

Am I happy? Am I healthy? How does my body really feel?"

If you can answer these in 2 minutes – you are more balanced than most.

However, *feeling* answers are **more**

important than simply stating the words.

Take the next 8 minutes noticing how your body feels. Just focus on each body part one by one -slowly. *Slowly* is the key word.

First notice your right eye, then your left eye. Notice how your lips feel, then the right and left ears. How about your neck? Bring your focus to each body part as you go along.

Notice your right upper arm, then the left upper arm- moving down to each wrist, hand and fingers. Then trail back-up into the main body at your chest -then slowly move to each and every body part. One by one. **Notice** how relaxed you feel by the time you get to your last little toe. This is **noticeable action.**

I am concluding this book. I am **noticing** that all of you are relaxed and balanced. Now you totally understand how you can meditate easily- better, **without a thought**!

Go meditate- already!

Here is *just a little somethin' about me and my writing.*

This book is a piece of eight. Sounds odd, Hugh?

What does that mean to you?

 To me it means infinity of many things, but currently it is the name of my mini book series.

Yeahas, 8 mini books. These pieces of 8 will advance your lives.

Oh crap! I went over 33 pages in this one.

Each mini book has 33 pages of content that *get right to the point* of what you want to know. I realize when you are searching for knowledge you run into a lot of fluff. Stuff like advertising or other crap takes over the real point of why you were searching for the information in the first place. I find most of the fluff- can be quite annoying.

I proclaim- let's *just* get to the good stuff!

Ergo the 8!   Enjoy friends!

Gratitude ~ Jolie DeMarco

We are all Souls that Live Together©

www.JolieDeMarco.com

Learn from videos at YouTube Jolie DeMarco

channel

www.ingramcontent.com/pod-product-compliance
Lightning Source LLC
Chambersburg PA
CBHW071127280526
45787CB00003B/1200